Michael Collins
The Big Fellow

Written by Rod Smith
and illustrated by Derry Dillon

IRELAND'S BEST KNOWN STORIES
IN A
NUTSHELL

Published 2016
Poolbeg Press Ltd

123 Grange Hill, Baldoyle
Dublin 13, Ireland

Text © Poolbeg Press Ltd 2016

A catalogue record for this book is available from the British Library.

ISBN 978 1 78199 875 5

Cover design and illustrations by Derry Dillon
Printed by GPS Colour Graphics Ltd, Alexander Road, Belfast BT6 9HP

This book belongs to

- -

The 6 Counties of
Northern Ireland

DONEGAL

DERRY

ANTRIM

Belfast

TYRONE

FERMANAGH

ARMAGH

DOWN

MONAGHAN

SLIGO

LEITRIM

CAVAN

MAYO

LOUTH

ROSCOMMON

Granard

LONGFORD

IRISH SEA

MEATH

WESTMEATH

DUBLIN

WALES

GALWAY

OFFALY

KILDARE

LAOIS

WICKLOW

CLARE

TIPPERARY

CARLOW

KILKENNY

LIMERICK

WEXFORD

WATERFORD

KERRY

CORK

Cloughduv

Macroom

Cork City

Béal na Bláth

Sam's
Cross

Bandon

Clonakilty

Available in the In a Nutshell Heroes Series

Pádraig Pearse and the Easter Rising 1916
Countess Markievicz — An Adventurous Life
James Connolly — Working Class Hero
Roger Casement — Human Rights Hero

"Ah, there you are, Michael!" his mother said as she saw her young son approaching the family farm. "Where have you been?"

"I was out walking."

"You do like those long walks, don't you? What's that book you're carrying today? Dickens? Shakespeare?"

"No, Mother – today it's one about Thomas Davis."

"And what do you think of him?"

"I think he was a great man. He wrote the words to the song 'A Nation Once Again' and he thought that people of different religions should work together to make an Ireland to be proud of."

"Well said, lad. Now, come on, enough reading for today! There's a lot of work to be done. First of all, I need you to milk the cows."

"That's fine with me," Michael said. "I may be small, but I'm not afraid of hard work!"

"No wonder your father used to call you 'Big Fellow'!" she said, laughing.

As they walked along together, Michael said, "Mam, I was reading about Arthur Griffith too and how he founded the Sinn Féin party. I wrote an essay about him."

"Did you now? And what did you say about him?"

"I said '*In Arthur Griffith there is a mighty force afoot in Ireland.*' And I said that he has a lot of wisdom and awareness of things which *are* Ireland."

His mother looked at him in astonishment – and not for the first time. Her youngest son was so clever and such a deep thinker. But she just said: "You don't say! Go on then — those cows won't milk themselves!"

Your father was right when he said that one day you will do great things for Ireland, his mother thought as Michael headed for the cowshed.

At the age of sixteen, Michael left school and joined the British Civil Service. Of course Ireland was part of Britain at that time. He went to work in the same Post Office Savings Bank in London where his older sister Hannie worked. His mother died the first week that he was away and poor Michael didn't have enough money to travel back for the funeral.

While he was in England he joined the Irish Republican Brotherhood, whose aim was to create an independent government in Ireland, free from British rule. They were prepared to use violence if necessary.

In London Michael became friendly with Sam Maguire and Liam McCarthy, both involved in the GAA (Gaelic Athletic Association) in London. Their names are well known now from the GAA all-Ireland football and hurling trophies. Michael also joined the Gaelic League and Sinn Féin. The Gaelic League worked on promoting Irish culture – that is, the Irish language and Irish music, games, drama, writing, folklore and art. Sinn Féin, which means 'We Ourselves', was a political party which wanted Irish freedom from Britain.

Michael travelled back to Dublin in 1916 when he heard that the Easter Rising was about to take place. He was the assistant to one of the leaders, Joseph Plunkett, who helped to plan the Rising. He was based in the GPO and helped to build barricades in the streets to block the British forces from getting near.

"Michael, I want you to guard the Telegraph Instrument Room," Joseph ordered.

"Is this all there is for me to do?" Michael wondered.

Then, when fire broke out in the GPO because of all the bombs that were being fired from the British gunship *Helga*, Michael tried to put the fires out. He burned his trousers while trying to do this.

Michael always had a great sense of humour. During the fighting he asked the leader Pádraig Pearse if he could leave the GPO for a short time.

"I promised some people I'd meet them for dinner," he said. "I'd hate to let them down!"

Pearse refused his request!

"Just as well, I suppose," said Michael. "I can't go to dinner with burnt trousers!"

When the Irish rebels surrendered, Michael was arrested along with the others.

As he stood with the Irish Volunteers, a British sergeant who knew him approached.

"What has you here, Collins?"

"England's difficulty!"

The Irish Volunteers all laughed. They knew he was referring to the saying "England's difficulty is Ireland's opportunity!" and the fact that England was at that time fighting against Germany in the Great War, which was later known as World War I.

As they were escorted to the boats, to be taken to Frongoch prison in Wales, they were pelted with rotten eggs and tomatoes by the women of Dublin. This was because their sons and husbands were fighting in the British army in the war and they relied on the army pay that was being sent back to Dublin.

Michael was not upset by this. He whistled the Cork tune, "The Banks of My Own Lovely Lee", as he walked.

His cousin Nancy had been looking for him in the crowd of prisoners and recognised the whistling.

"Michael Collins, what has you so cheerful?" she called out.

"Ah, Nancy, don't worry! We'll be ready for the next round against the British and this time we'll win!"

At the Frongoch prison camp in Wales, Michael quickly became one of the leaders of the prisoners. He encouraged the men to refuse to give their names to the guards which led to lots of confusion. Meetings were organised where information was exchanged.

"The British have made a big mistake putting us all together in one place," he said to the men one day.

"What do you mean?"

"This prison camp has become a university for the Irish rebels. We are learning so much from one another. The Easter Rising was a disaster. There was courage and loyalty, but no organisation. We won't make the same mistakes next time."

Michael was very competitive when playing sports and hated to lose. At Frongoch he won the 100-yard sprint and came second in the weight-throwing competition.

When the prisoners were released in December 1916, Michael travelled around England encouraging people to support the cause of Irish independence. Guns were hidden in egg-boxes and sent to Ireland by supporters in England!

In 1917 Michael fell in love with a girl from Granard, Longford, called Kitty Kiernan. They wrote hundreds of letters to one another over the next few years.

When Sinn Féin won the general election in 1918 it declared Ireland a republic. Éamon De Valera became the first president of the Irish parliament, which they called the Dáil. Michael became Commander-in-Chief of the army and the Minister for Finance.

The first Dáil meeting took place on the 21st
January 1919. On the same day, the shooting of two
policemen led to the beginning of the Anglo-Irish
War against the British which lasted until 1921.

Michael set up a spy network called "The Squad"
to spy on and carry out attacks on the British.

Michael met with other leaders to give them their orders.

"This war will be different. We won't be a target
that stands still. We will attack and move. That way
they can send all the gunships and troops that they
want and they won't be able to find us."

Special units called "Flying Columns" were created to fight in this way, attacking and moving on before they could be captured.

At the time, there were two police forces in Ireland: one in Dublin and the Royal Irish Constabulary (RIC) for the rest of the country.

A Dublin police officer was captured for spying on the Irish. Michael tied him to a railing.

"We're not going to hurt you. We have many friends and relations in the Dublin police force. We're here to give you a warning. We do what we do for Ireland's freedom. If you do not want to help, then do not hinder."

"Well, it's very decent of you not to shoot me," the policeman replied. "You have my word I won't do anything against you."

Soon members of the Dublin police force began to provide Michael with information about British agents who were operating in Dublin.

Outside Dublin, Michael decided to strike against the RIC.

"They control the small towns and villages. If we target them, we'll get the support of the Irish people. We will also get the weapons they have stored in their stations."

Attacks started around the country and, on Easter Sunday 1920, many police stations were burned down.

The British forces hunted for Michael but could not find him.

One day, Emmet Dalton, a good friend of his, arrived with a file with the name '*Michael Collins*' on it.

"It's the intelligence file the British have on you," he said.

Michael opened it.

"Michael Collins. Wanted by the British. Born in Cork. Height 6 feet 4 inches. Intelligent, young and powerful. No photograph available."

"What! 6 feet 4 inches! I'm only five feet eleven inches tall!"

"What about the 'intelligent, young and powerful' part?"

"A perfect description of me!" Michael said, laughing.

"They don't know what you look like, and they can't find you. They're calling you the Irish Pimpernel!"

"So, they're comparing me to the fellow in the books, the Scarlet Pimpernel – the famous lord who saved people from execution during the French Revolution and could never be found! Well, I am no lord. I walk around in ordinary clothes, and cycle around Dublin on my bike, so they won't know it's me!"

British Prime Minister David Lloyd George sent over two new police forces to help the RIC: the Auxiliary Division and the Black and Tans.

'Black and Tans' was actually a nickname given by the Irish to that group of soldiers. This was because they didn't wear proper uniforms with matching colours and that reminded people of black-and-tan beagle dogs. They were hated throughout the land because of their harsh methods of dealing with people.

Michael was having dinner in a restaurant in Dublin one day when it was raided by the British forces.

"You are Michael Collins!" one of them said.

"No, I am John Grace," he calmly replied, and produced documentation to show that this was the case. He was not arrested.

However, Éamon de Valera was caught and sent to Lincoln prison in England. However, Michael later helped him to escape.

At another time, Michael was having a meeting with other leaders in a Dublin hotel when they heard the screech of brakes. Michael ran to the window. A Black and Tan convoy had pulled up outside. Michael laughed. "These fellows are only raiding the house next door!"

On the 21st November 1920 Michael ordered an attack on British spies. Fifteen people were killed.

That same afternoon, the British forces went to Croke Park and fired into the crowd at a Dublin–Tipperary football match. Fourteen people were killed, including Tipperary player Michael Hogan, after whom the Hogan Stand in Croke Park is named. Over sixty people were wounded.

Éamon de Valera arrived back from America where he had been trying to raise funds and get support for the Irish cause.

"How are things going?" he asked.

"Great! The Big Fellow is leading us and everything is marvellous!"

De Valera grew angry. "We'll see who's the Big Fellow!"

He met with Michael.

"We need to show the British that we are strong. Then they'll ask for a treaty," de Valera said. "We need a major military operation in Dublin."

"We don't have the numbers, Éamon. The British have almost twelve thousand troops and police in the city. We have two thousand, and only a few hundred of them are trained to fight. Besides, we are very short on ammunition."

Nevertheless, de Valera insisted and an attack on the Custom House was carried out on the 25th May 1921. The attempt to burn it down was unsuccessful and over one hundred Irish volunteers were arrested. This defeat seriously weakened the Irish forces.

However, by this time, Archbishop Clune of Australia was involved in talks between the Irish and the British about a possible treaty.

He met the British Prime Minister, Lloyd George, to discuss the matter.

"The Irish rebels are a bunch of assassins!" Lloyd George declared.

"Not so, Prime Minister. They are the cream of their race."

"How do you get to meet that Collins chap when my own Secret Service cannot find him?"

"I meet him whenever I wish. I catch a train to a particular train station and there is always someone on the platform who whispers an address to me as he passes me by."

Lloyd George laughed. "Very clever! Let's arrange a meeting to discuss treaty terms."

Michael met a senior British civil servant, Andy Cope, to discuss arrangements.

"At last we meet face to face," smirked Mr Cope. "I hear I am number one on your list of people who should be shot."

"Not at all, Mr. Cope – you're only number three on the list!"

Michael reported back to de Valera.

"I want you to go over to London to negotiate terms with the British," de Valera told Michael.

"What do I know about negotiating with politicians?" said Michael. "I am a soldier. You should go. You're our best negotiator."

"No, I am your president and a president shouldn't be part of those kinds of discussions. I want you to go with Arthur Griffith and take care of this for me."

Michael reluctantly agreed.

"They'll say it's your fault if anything goes wrong," warned his friend Emmet Dalton.

"Let them blame me if they like. Someone must go. Let's have a plane ready over there, just in case they try to arrest me and I need to make a quick escape!"

Michael became engaged to Kitty Kiernan just before he travelled to London.

Talks between the British and Irish negotiators were difficult and took place over a number of months.

Eventually a truce was agreed and signed by both parties. The Free State of Ireland was created with 26 counties. The 6 counties in Northern Ireland would remain in the United Kingdom which was what most of the people in the north wanted.

"I may have signed my political death warrant tonight," said Lord Birkenhead, one of the British representatives.

"I may have signed my actual death warrant," Michael replied.

Back in Ireland, Michael started to receive threatening letters and phone calls, accusing him of betraying Ireland and selling out to the British.

Countess Markievicz, one of the leaders of the Easter 1916 Rising was very unhappy. "Michael Collins, you are a traitor. I do not think much of this treaty you have signed."

"Countess, we welcome opposition, peaceful opposition. Remember, this is just the first step to full independence."

"I think you got a little bit too cosy and comfortable with the British and it affected your judgement."

"Well, let's put it to a vote, and let the members of Dáil decide."

Dáil Éireann voted by a narrow margin to agree to the Treaty. Éamon de Valera refused to accept this and walked out.

Two groups were created. The group who supported the Treaty was called the Regulars. The group against the Treaty was called the Irregulars. Fighting broke out between the two. The Irish Civil War had begun.

Michael, who was a powerful passionate speaker, travelled to places around the country, speaking in support of the Treaty to huge crowds of people.

When Michael was arriving at a meeting in Dublin, a young man ran up to him as he got out of his car and shot him at point-blank range. The man was so nervous that he missed and Michael was unharmed.

Even though Michael could lose his temper from time to time, at this moment his kind and thoughtful personality shone through. "Don't arrest him," he said. "He has a good face. Send him home to his mother!"

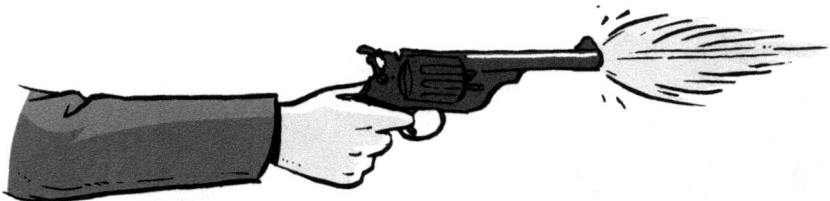

Arthur Griffith had become a good friend of Michael's. Then in August 1922, he had a heart attack and died.

Arthur had great respect for Michael: "I have no ambition that my name go down in Irish History," he said, "but if it does I want it to be associated with the name Michael Collins."

Shortly after Arthur's death, Michael decided to travel down to Cork where a lot of people were against the Treaty.

"Are you sure it's a good idea to go there?" Emmet Dalton asked. "It may not be safe."

"I don't suppose I will be ambushed in my own county," said Michael.

They stopped at Clonakilty for lunch where Michael saw one of the soldiers who was against the Treaty. "It's too bad he's on the other side now," he said, "because he's a fine soldier."

As Michael and his convoy passed an area called Béal na Bláth they were attacked.

"Drive on! Get us out of here!" Emmet shouted to the driver.

"No! Let's get out and fight!" Michael ordered.

The car stopped and he jumped out. Light was fading so it was hard to see exactly what was going on. Michael ran around a corner of the road, gun in hand, firing shots towards his attackers.

Emmet Dalton and another friend of Michael's called Seán O'Connell finally caught up with him and found him lying on the road. He had been shot and was not moving. Seán held his hand and said a prayer. Michael squeezed his hand gently and looked towards Emmet.

"Emmet . . ." he said as he breathed his last.

He was only 31 years old and was due to marry Kitty Kiernan later that year.

Michael was the only person killed in the ambush. To this day there is still a lot of discussion about who fired the shot that killed him. Some locals claim they know who did it, and say that this person visited the Collins family home afterwards and apologised for the shooting.

His body was brought to a small church at Cloughduv near Cork where a priest administered the Last Rites. He was then brought to a hospital where he was laid out in his uniform. Candles were lit in the room.

Michael's death was greeted with shock throughout Ireland and Britain.

"My God, that is too bad. There's no hope for peace now," said de Valera when he heard the news.

Tom Barry, who had been fighting against Michael and was now in Kilmainham Gaol, looked out of his cell window into the yard below. He later said, "I looked down from my high cell and saw over seven hundred men kneeling and praying for Collins, and he the one who put them there."

The English newspaper, *The Daily Telegraph*, wrote: "He was the stuff of which great men are made."

Michael's coffin was transported by boat to Dublin. Father Doyle, a friend of Michael's, said "A cry of agony broke from the throats of strong men" as the coffin arrived.

Thousands lined the streets of Dublin on the day of the funeral.

Michael was buried in Glasnevin Cemetery. General Richard Mulcahy, who was made Commander-in-Chief after Michael's death, spoke over his grave. He said: "He made himself a hero and a legend that will stand in the pages of our history with any bright page that was ever written there."

The Civil War finally ended in 1923 when the Anti-Treaty fighters dumped their arms and stopped fighting. It had been a bitter struggle. Almost two thousand people had been killed.

Many years later, when De Valera was president of the Irish Republic, he spoke of the legacy of Michael Collins: "It's my considered opinion that in the fullness of time, history will record the greatness of Collins and it will be recorded at my expense."

To this day, the grave of Michael Collins is one of the most popular attractions at Glasnevin cemetery, especially on Valentine's Day. Kitty Kiernan was buried near his grave when she died in 1945. Later she had married someone else but named her second son 'Michael Collins'.

A few days after his death, the famous playwright George Bernard Shaw wrote to Michael's sister Hannie to pay his respects:

"I met Michael for the first and last time on Saturday last. I am very glad I did. I rejoice in his memory. So tear up your mourning and hang up your brightest colours in his honour."

The End

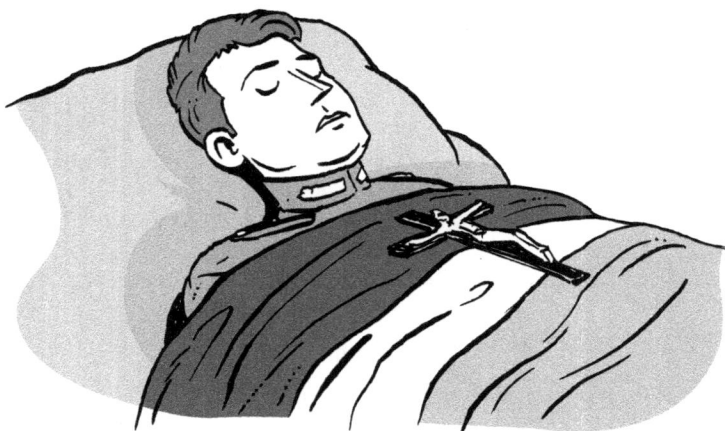

from **The Mouth of Flowers**

They left his blossom, white and slender
Beneath Glasnevin's shaking sod;
His spirit passed like sunset splendour
Unto the dead Fiannas' God.

Good luck be with you, Michael Collins,
Or stay or go you far away;
Or stay you with the folk of fairy,

Or come with ghosts another day.

(By Sir Shane Leslie, after seeing a painting
of the dead Michael Collins by Sir John Lavery)

GLOSSARY *(alphabetical order)*

administered: to hand out or give something in an official way

afoot: happening or about to happen

assassin: a person who attacks and kills by surprise

auxiliary: giving help or support

beagle: a small hunting dog. Normally white, black and light brown/tan in colour

Béal na Bláth: a small village in West Cork. The name could mean "the mouth of the flowers" or possibly "the mouth of the buttermilk"

Civil Service: organisation of people responsible for helping the government run the country from day to day

Dáil: Parliament of the Irish Republic

death warrant: a document giving official permission for the execution of a condemned person

finance: managing money or helping to raise money

folklore: stories, beliefs and customs told by word of mouth from generation to generation

margin: the edge or border of something ('by a narrow margin' means 'by a very small amount')

negotiate: to have talks in order to come to an agreement

network: a group of connected people or things

opportunity: a chance

point-blank: aimed or fired at very close range

Scarlet Pimpernel: a small red flower that closes its petals and 'hides' in wet weather and at different times of the day. Name given to the hero of the books by Emma Orczy because he was a master of disguise.

treaty: a signed agreement between two countries

Some Things to Talk About

1. What kinds of books did Michael like to read?
2. What did Michael think of Arthur Griffith?
3. Where did Michael go to work when he was 16?
4. What did Michael do during the 1916 Easter Rising?
5. Can you give some examples of Michael's sense of humour?
6. Why did Michael think the British made a mistake putting the Irish prisoners all together at Frongoch prison camp?
7. What mistakes did Michael think the rebels made in the Easter Rising in 1916?
8. Why was Michael friendly with the police in Dublin, and not friendly with the police outside Dublin?
9. Why did the British forces find it so difficult to track Michael down?
10. What orders did Michael give to his agents on the 21st November 1920?
11. What did the British forces do in Croke Park in revenge?
12. Were Michael and Éamon de Valera good friends?
13. Why do you think de Valera sent Michael to London to negotiate the Anglo-Irish Treaty?
14. Why did Michael say he was signing his death warrant when he signed the Anglo-Irish Treaty?
15. Why was there an Irish Civil War?
16. What happened to Michael's good friend Arthur Griffith that upset Michael?
17. What happened on the night Michael was killed?
18. What do you think might have happened in Irish history if Michael had lived?
19. Have you ever visited Michael's grave at Glasnevin?

Timeline

1890: Michael born in West Cork, near Clonakilty

1906: Goes to work for Post Office in London

1909: Joins the Irish Republican Brotherhood

1916: Returns to Ireland
Assistant to Joseph Plunkett in the Easter Rising
Arrested and gaoled in Frongoch prison camp in Wales

1918: Helps de Valera escape from Lincoln prison in England
Elected as Member of Parliament for Cork
Sinn Féin wins 73 seats in the General Election

1919: First Dáil meets and declares independence from Britain
Michael becomes Head of the Irish Army and Minister for Finance
Beginning of Anglo-Irish War

1920: British spies killed and football supporters at Dublin–Tipperary
match shot in revenge on 21st November

1921: Irish forces attack the Custom House in Dublin
Anglo-Irish Treaty agreed between Ireland and Britain
26 counties become Irish Free State, 6 counties remain in the UK

1922: Irish Civil War begins between groups for and against the Treaty
Michael killed at an ambush at Béal na Bláth, West Cork, near Clonakilty
Buried at Glasnevin Cemetery, Dublin

1923: Irish Civil War ends

1945: Michael's fiancée Kitty Kiernan dies and is buried near Michael's grave at
Glasnevin

1949: 26 counties of the Irish Free State become the Republic of Ireland

2014: The Glasnevin Trust confirms that many cards and flowers are still sent
to Michael Collins' grave every Valentine's Day